THINK LIKE A
HEADHUNTER

THE CFO'S GUIDE TO
THE HIDDEN JOB MARKET

Lance Osborne

ISBN 978-1-988360-04-1 (paperback)
ISBN 978-1-988360-05-8 (ePUB)

Cover design, and interior typesetting:
Daniel Crack, Kinetics Design, kdbooks.ca
linkedin.com/in/kdbooks

CONTENTS

Introduction 5

1 The Healthy but Hidden Market for CFOs 9

2 A Surprising Look at How Most CFOs Are Actually Hired 17

3 A Stroll Down the Path of Least Resistance 24

4 Resumes: Stock the Shelves with the Stuff That Sells 33

5 Switching Industries 41

6 Prepping for the Interview 47

7 Avoiding the Bad Bosses 55

8 What You Need to Know About Headhunters 61

9 Putting It All Together 68

Afterword 73

Appendix A More Straight Answers to Real Questions 75

Appendix B About Osborne Financial Search 91

Introduction

I've learned in my 30 years of executive search that financial executives are good at a lot of things. "Need to develop a performance measuring system covering asset utilization, operational performance and return on investment? Not a problem." "Company needs to put some debt financing in place? Should have that for you by the end of the month." "Thinking of installing a new ERP system? Let's meet after lunch."

By the time someone has percolated up through the ranks to finally sit in the CFO chair, they have lots of experience with and are thoroughly competent in any number of technical and operational matters. However, every now and again, a senior financial executive has to deal with what can sometimes be a brand new issue, one they usually have virtually no experience with – looking for a new job.

Of course, everyone has some job-hunting experience, but looking for a new position when the ink's still wet on your accounting designation certificate is an entirely different proposition than looking for a new gig from the lofty heights of the executive suite. Back when you were an aspiring and promising young accounting professional, jobs were plentiful and whoever ended up hiring you wasn't taking that much of a risk by putting you on the payroll. No doubt they wanted you to succeed but if you didn't perform as you should, not that much harm was done and you were relatively easy to replace.

If you did perform as promised or even excelled (which we're assuming you did since you made it to CFO), then odds are that was the one and only time you were actively looking for a new job. After that, the succession of jobs on your road to CFO most likely came to you in one form or another. Even if you decided to initiate the process somewhere along the line, that probably entailed talking to a couple of headhunters and maybe applying to select job postings and then sitting back and waiting for the ball to start rolling.

Let's say you're a gainfully employed and somewhat (if not outrageously) happy CFO who would like to move if the right opportunity presents itself in the next year or two. Your previous game plan of talking to a couple of headhunters and responding to plum job postings is still a viable strategy. However, if you're actively unhappy in your current position, if you're unemployed, or if your Spidey-sense is telling you that you're going to be on the street sometime in the next 12 months, you need a whole different strategy to find yourself a new home in a reasonable time frame.

Looking for a job as a CFO is a very different matter than looking for a job as a financial analyst or assistant controller.

- **The stakes are different – they're much greater for both you and your prospective employer.**

- **The process is different – people hiring more junior accounting professionals are filling a function, people hiring a CFO are impacting their company.**

- **The market is different – jobs are plentiful and well advertised for the rookie; they seem to be more scarce and often hidden from view for financial executives.**

- **The timelines are different – instead of finding a new position in a matter of a month or two, CFOs often need to budget six months to a year (or more) to find a good position (emphasis on *good*, bad positions take much less time to find).**

This guide provides an overview of the job market for CFOs and practical advice on how to go about finding your next position. In a perfect world, applying these principles and following the tactics I outline will help you find your dream job. But if nothing else, my goal is to help you materially shorten the time you spend looking for your next position.

1

The Healthy but Hidden Market for CFOs

When you were a bright, young, up and coming accounting professional, you probably thought that the job market was pretty good, even hot at times. Excepting the 1990-1992 recession, your impression would have been that the demand for people like you and your cohort was constant and consistent. Job boards would have been full of ads relating to jobs in budget analysis, management reporting, audit, financial reporting and a host of other finance and accounting positions. Your phone would have rung with great regularity with recruiters of all stripes trying to discern if you might be interested in making a move. Apocryphal stories would circulate of someone specializing in the high-tech sector at Ernst & Young or PwC making a move to an internet startup for a package that was more than double their compensation in public accounting.

Options were plentiful at this age and stage, and you probably made your first, second and maybe even third career moves without ever having to do anything other than respond to whatever next best opportunity the headhunter happened to approach you on. Based on this kind of experience in your early career, you may have made the assumption that the same cornucopia of opportunities exists for you today. However, as much as you may have been the belle of the ball twenty years ago, you're probably noticing that available opportunities today seem much fewer and farther between.

That's because the market for CFOs is very different from the market for more junior financial professionals. The differences in these markets has to do with frequency of demand and the visibility of the available positions.

Once companies hire their tranche of entry-level accounting professionals, they've got an internal bench of talent. Although they may have had to hire from outside for an open financial analyst position, they can promote from within when the manager of financial reporting position opens up. If and when a large, well-run company hires at the executive level, they have a deep bench to draw upon so they usually don't need to go outside to hire. The jobs are there; they just get filled internally.

And finance executives tend to stay in their positions longer so there is less churn in the top end of the market. On average, people in financial analysis, financial reporting and internal audit positions change employers every three years or so. By contrast, a report by Spencer Stuart had the average CFO tenure for Fortune 500 companies at 5.9 years. There's very little reliable data on the average tenure of CFOs in small and medium-sized enterprises (SMEs), but anecdotally, I would put that number at about eight years.

Finally, the demand curve for finance professionals shifts as they become more senior. The majority of qualified accounting professionals start their careers with very large companies but most of them find themselves working for much smaller organizations in the later stages of their careers.

And when you think about it, it makes a lot of sense. Large corporations are necessarily hierarchical. There's a CFO at the top of the finance organizational chart and hundreds of junior people at the bottom. As a financial professional starts getting promoted, there are fewer and fewer positions available to them as they progress up the ranks.

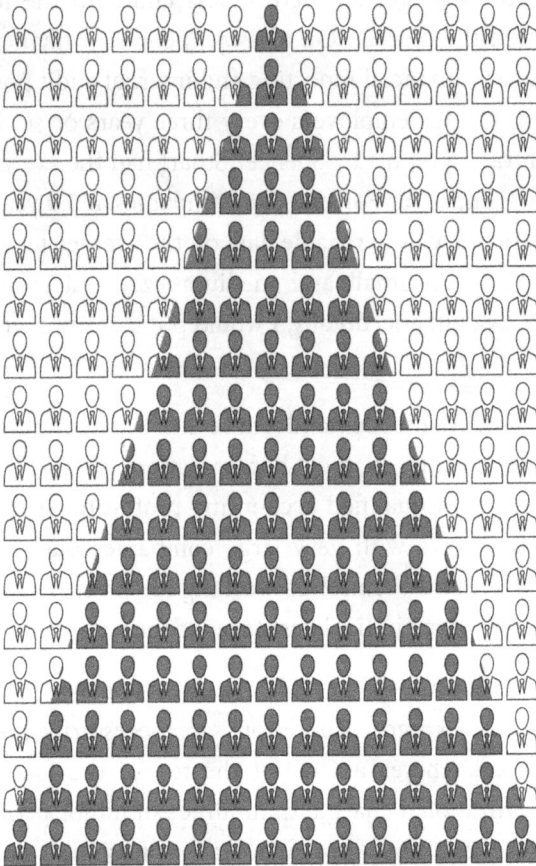

Figure 1

Let's represent the entire market of large companies as being one company. And let's assume that that company hires 100 young accountants on the same day. Let's also assume that these people all have the capability of progressing through the ranks at an equal pace.

As you can see from Figure 1, as this cohort marches from the bottom to the top, the number of positions filled by these people in this particular organization gets smaller and smaller, but the absolute number of the cohort remains the same.

By the time they get to the top of the organizational chart, only one of the accountants who started with the company is left.

So what happened to the other 99?

Well, for the most part, the rest of this cohort ended up in SMEs. Which isn't surprising, since SMEs by far comprise the biggest employment sector in Canada. According to our friends at Industry Canada, firms with 500 or more employees are referred to as "large businesses," and the term SME is applied to businesses with fewer than 500 employees.

Of course, 1 to 499 employees covers a lot of ground, so Industry Canada further defines a small business as one with fewer than 100 employees if it produces goods or as having fewer than 50 employees if it's a service-based business.

To define small business even further, we can roughly apply the Industry Canada revenue per employee figure (manufacturing sector) of $400,000. So a typical manufacturer with 50 employees will have revenues of about $20mm, and one with 300 employees may have revenues of about $120mm.

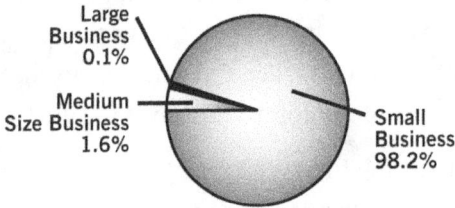

Figure 2 – Canadian Business Market by Employee Size

Large Business 0.1%

Medium Size Business 1.6%

Small Business 98.2%

Another interesting statistic, courtesy of Industry Canada, is that broken down by number of employees, small businesses make up 98.2% of the market, with medium-sized businesses at 1.6% of employer businesses and large businesses at 0.1%.

Because very large companies have a constant and steady appetite for entry-level finance and accounting professionals, they comprise the biggest part of the job market for those people. However, as those entry level financial professionals progress up the career ladder, there are fewer and fewer senior-level positions in those large companies to accommodate them.

So, in order to get a bigger job, senior finance professionals and executives often need to move to a smaller firm where all of the higher-end, value-add finance functions are handled by the CFO.

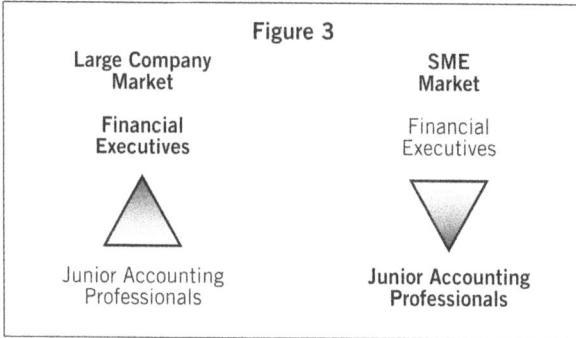

Figure 3

Large Company Market — Financial Executives / Junior Accounting Professionals

SME Market — Financial Executives / Junior Accounting Professionals

Just as there's a healthy market for junior accounting professionals in large corporations, there's also a healthy market for CFOs in the SME market. The big difference between the two is in how large companies recruit and how smaller companies recruit. When large companies need to go to the outside market to find someone, the position they're trying to fill is typically very well broadcast. When SMEs need to recruit, the positions are very poorly broadcast, so the vast majority of CFO positions that become available are largely hidden from view. It is estimated that as many as 85% of available CFO roles are never made public in any meaningful way.

Whether you're a senior financial executive in a FP 500 company or a Vice President, Finance in an SME, if you're thinking about making a career change, accessing this hidden job market for CFOs should be an integral part of your job-search strategy.

Straight Answers to Real Questions

▶ **Lost in Translation?**

Question: I have over 20 years' experience as a finance professional and like to think that I've excelled at every position and every company that I've been a part of. I've spent most of my career in the food service industry and I'm looking for my next challenge. I've applied to a number of CFO positions outside of the food service industry that I feel I'm very well qualified for but I'm not making any headway. Am I stuck in this industry for the rest of my professional life or can I take my career in another direction?

Answer: When companies first go to market for any position, especially the CFO spot, significant experience in their particular industry is usually at the very top of their list of qualification criteria. If they can't find exact industry experience, the hiring authority's next choice will be well-qualified candidates from industries with issues and challenges analogous to their industry. Take a hard look at the business and financial issues you've had to deal with in the food service business and figure out what other industries they may apply to. If you can articulate how your experience translates directly into other industries, it should dramatically broaden the pool of companies that will consider you to be a viable candidate.

2

A Surprising Look at How Most CFOs Are Actually Hired

Any financial executive who has spent any time in a large corporate environment is very familiar with the drill when it comes to hiring for the management or executive ranks. The process starts with a thorough review of the position, including the function being served, how the position fits in the grand scheme of things and how all stakeholders are impacted by the position. Consideration is given to current corporate culture, what kind of management style would work best, expected tenure in the position, the potential to grow within the position and the potential to eventually move out of that job to something bigger and better within the company.

Once the position has been thoroughly scoped out, a detailed candidate profile is created covering all the technical, operational, management experience and personality characteristics required to succeed in the position and in the company.

After the position description and preferred candidate profile have been documented, the next step is to decide how to go about recruiting for the position. All large corporations have human resources departments that are usually called in to assist with the search. These human resources departments often have specialized talent acquisition professionals who will sometimes conduct the search themselves. More commonly at the executive level, human resources will enlist the aid of an executive search firm.

The executive search firm will then come up with a search strategy. This strategy will include advertising the position online and in print and scanning their internal candidate database. The biggest component of the headhunter's strategy will be researching and mapping out the topography of the potential candidate pool that they will then call to recruit on their client's behalf.

So, if a headhunter has a CFO search assignment for their widget manufacturing client and you're the VP Finance in a good size widget company, your profile will show up on the headhunter's hit list. And if you look like you might have the goods, rest assured you'll be getting a call.

Once the executive recruiter has gone through their process, they will have probably considered hundreds of potential candidates, reached out to scores of them, interviewed 10 or more and eventually narrowed those potential candidates down to a short list of four or five.

If the headhunter has done their job right, most, if not all financial executives in the Canadian widget space will have either seen the position in the *Globe and Mail* or the *National Post*, run across the posting on LinkedIn, or had a call from a recruiter trying to recruit them or looking for a referral.

The short list is presented to the client, interviews are conducted and, after what is usually a very rigorous if not exhausting exercise in due diligence by all parties, the widget company hires its new CFO.

If you've been through the process either as a hiring authority or a candidate, you'd be forgiven for assuming that every company went through a similar process when hiring a CFO.

But surprisingly, unlike much larger organizations, there's no equivalent protocol for hiring executives in SMEs. A CEO in this market who needs to recruit a CFO may start the search by asking for a referral from their public accounting firm. If that approach doesn't turn anyone up, they'll probably ask around their social and business networks to see if those people know of anyone. They might also put out feelers to anyone they know professionally or personally who happens to be a CPA. And of course, if they're plugged into LinkedIn and the need to fill the position is urgent, they'll often post the job there as well.

These tactics will produce candidates. The public accounting firms would be delighted to plug an alumnus into that job, guaranteeing that the client stays a client. And the owner-manager's professional contacts, friends and neighbours will usually know a senior finance person who needs a new gig.

As we'll discuss in Chapter 3, in many cases, the need to hire a CFO isn't all that pressing, so the owner-manager or CEO of the SME doing the recruiting won't post the position on a job board unless their networking efforts come up completely short and they're under the gun to hire. But the window the hiring authority is working with is usually months long, so the odds are pretty good that word of mouth will produce some viable candidates.

Because these available jobs are not widely broadcast, most of the finance executives who should have heard about that position did not and will not. You may be the absolutely perfect fit for any number of CFO positions that arise every year, but unless you're very lucky, chances are that you won't hear about any of them.

Which is a real shame because not only are you missing out on good opportunities, the CEOs doing the hiring are missing out as well. They probably won't end up hiring someone terrible but they could have done much better – they could have hired you.

Straight Answers to Real Questions

▶ *Fool Me Once*

Question: I started with my current firm as Director of Finance six months ago, reporting directly to the CEO who is also the owner of the company. The company had gone through two other Directors of Finance in the four years previous and the company's finances and finance department were in a state of total disarray. I was told during the interview process by both the recruiter and the CEO that I would be free to make any changes I saw fit. In fact, I was told specifically that I was being hired because they needed a real change agent in the top finance job. I was excited by the opportunity to make a real difference when I joined the firm but now, six months later, I'm totally frustrated. Having given me the mandate to overhaul the finance group, the CEO is either stalling on or vetoing every initiative I've proposed. Just to name a few, he won't let me fire the accounting manager (his wife's cousin), implement a new ERP system (too expensive/disruptive) or establish performance metrics for the operations side of the business (other executives would find them too intrusive).

I really need to get out of here but I'm afraid of being burned again. How can I ensure next time out that the job I'm interviewing for is the job I actually get?

Answer: Every situation is different, but in any and all situations where you're considering joining a new company, you need to do your own due diligence.

People tend to hear what they want to hear and will overlook discrepancies in the story they're being told if they like the overall story. Take your current situation as an example. You liked the challenge of cleaning up the finance group, but didn't dig deep enough into how it came to be in such a bad state. No doubt, the CEO and/or recruiter characterized the situation as having been the fault of the previous two Directors of Finance, but bells should have been ringing, and ringing loudly. As tactfully as possible, you should have found out in detail how the previous incumbents handled the position and the specifics around them leaving the company (i.e. did they jump or were they pushed?). Even if you buy into the premise that the previous Directors were that bad, it implies that the CEO isn't all that adept at hiring finance executives. And if that's the case, you have to ask yourself why he would have any better luck with you.

The other possibility is that the fault doesn't lie with the other Directors of Finance at all, which means you need to find out what's really going on before you even think about signing on the dotted line. So, just as the company did reference checks on you, you should have done reference checks on them. The best tactic in this case would have been to contact the previous Directors on LinkedIn, tell them you're interviewing for their prior position and ask to speak with them on a confidential basis about the company and the job. In some cases when you take this tack, you might end up hearing excuses and sour grapes. However, in your case, I think you would have heard a lot of new information that would have had you running in the opposite direction.

3

A Stroll Down the Path of Least Resistance

What common theme do SMEs have when it comes to recruiting a CFO? They tend to take the path of least resistance.

Two factors come into play here. Factor number one is that the vast majority of SME CEOs come out of sales or operations, or they were born into the business. They typically have a detailed and thorough understanding of every facet of their business with the exception of finance and accounting. So they tend to be less rigorous in their recruiting of a financial executive than they would be of a sales or operations executive.

Factor number two is that like almost all executives, they hate the recruitment process. Done properly, it can be a very time consuming, expensive exercise and, if there's an easy way out of it, they'll usually take it.

When a CEO of an SME needs to recruit someone to head up their financial function, often their plan of attack is to reach out to their accounting firm partner for a referral, put the word out to their personal network and, if the demand is critical, i.e. the incumbent has just resigned, they'll post the position on a couple of job boards. The virtue of this approach is that they require very little investment, both in terms of time and money. The downside to this approach is that, as with most things, you get what you pay for.

Whatever one may think of the aforementioned "path of least resistance," it represents an opportunity for proactive financial executives who want to (or need to) turbo-charge their job-search efforts.

Start by plugging into the networks that will most likely be tapped by a CEO looking for a referral. Try to connect with public accounting partners, lawyers and bankers whose primary market is small and medium-sized enterprises. And make a point of reaching out to your peers who are perfectly happy in their current jobs but will be in a position to refer you on if a headhunter calls them. If there happens to be someone who has the inside track on your industry's goings-on, connect with them as well. These people could include subject matter experts, industry speakers and editors of industry trade magazines.

Job postings are an obvious venue for any job seeker. But you should be aware that companies only advertise positions when there is a sudden or critical need such as the resignation of an incumbent. This is the tip of the iceberg when it comes to the actual number of CFO positions actually available to you. For every CFO position being advertised because of a critical need, there are many more positions that could be available but aren't in the public domain because the need isn't as pressing.

For every company that's in the market for a new CFO due to an unexpected resignation, there's another company in the market for a new CFO because:

1. **The company's at a point where they need to hire their first qualified CFO.**

2. **The long-tenured incumbent will be retiring in the next 12 months.**

3. **The company needs to replace an underperforming incumbent.**

In these three instances, there's usually a matter of some months from when the company first realizes that they need to hire someone new to when they actually pull the trigger and initiate a search.

Owner-managers who need to hire their first CFO typically come to that decision quite slowly. Even after they've made the decision to fill this gap in their executive team, there's often a lot of soul searching over what they should be looking for in their first CFO. And by definition, if an owner-manager has made a decision to hire their first CFO, it's because their business has grown significantly in size and/or complexity. And because they're very busy and they know that recruiting a CFO will be a big time commitment, owner-managers will often procrastinate quite a bit before they finally decide to start the search.

An example of one of these kinds of out-of-sight CFO opportunities would be a small to medium-sized manufacturing concern whose operations require proper management of the infrastructure and financial discipline to take the company to the next level. The owner-manager knows they have to hire a proper Director or Vice President of Finance, but doesn't know how or where to look and so has been deferring doing anything about the position for the past six months.

Another good example would be one of the Canadian success stories featured in *Profit Magazine* about companies that have been enjoying five-year revenue growth on the order of 300% to 15,000%. You have to imagine that the CEO of a company experiencing revenue growth of 15,000% over the past five years is probably pretty busy. And even though they know that the controller they hired back when the company was small can't keep up with the company's growth, they dread the prospect of a lengthy, time-intensive executive search process involved in finding a qualified CFO.

CEOs who need to replace an underperforming incumbent also take a long time to pull the trigger on the actual decision. Sometimes they're hoping that the incumbent will improve and sometimes they're just reluctant to fire anyone until they have to. Most often, it's because the realization that they have a problem comes to them over a matter of many months, the issues gradually accumulating to the point where the CEO decides that they can't put the decision off any longer.

As I previously noted, many, if not most CEOs actively dislike the recruitment process and there is a natural tendency to defer it as long as possible. And since many CEOs would rather have their problem go away without having to engage in a full-blown executive search process, they'll often hire the first viable candidate that walks through the door. A big part of your job-hunting strategy should be to increase the odds that it's you who'd be walking through that door.

The key for a proactive job seeker is intelligent research and an equally intelligent (and compelling) pitch. The big thing you're looking for is evidence of change. Change in ownership, change in leadership, change in geography, change in market share, change in product offering – any major change in an organization can lead to changes in the organizational chart. Not always, not even usually, but sometimes these kinds of changes translate into opportunities.

One almost surefire indicator that there will be a CFO position available in the next year or so is if a private company is acquired by a private equity firm. According to a survey conducted by PwC, a private equity firm will replace the incumbent CFO of a newly acquired portfolio company in the first 12 months 70% of the time.

Here are the ground rules for research:

1. Gather high-quality sources that may point to companies of interest. There are numerous free online directories such as the *Report on Business Top 1000*, *Financial Post*'s FP 500 or *Branham300*. One of my favourites in this category is the *Profit 500* list of Canada's fastest growing companies.

2. Every industry has one or more dedicated trade magazines that cover current industry issues, companies on the way up, mergers and acquisitions and executives on the move. Trade magazines often have positions posted if they have an online version.

3. When possible, go apples to apples. If your background is primarily automobile parts manufacturing, you're probably wasting your time pitching to an up-and-coming high-tech startup.

4. Go to the prospect company's website and check out the management team. If the incumbent Vice President, Finance's bio suggests they're a recent hire or are obviously well suited to the position, move on. If their LinkedIn profile shows that the incumbent CFO changes jobs every two years or if the incumbent looks like they may be near retirement age, maybe there's an opportunity there. And if there's a controller listed but no VP Finance, that may represent an opportunity as well.

Investigate the specific issues a company may be experiencing as a function of its industry, competitive position in the marketplace or rate of growth. In a perfect world, you'll come up with a list of companies in your industry that have been experiencing dramatic growth and, as a result, could or should be considering a change in financial management.

Now all you have to do is send off your resumé with a cover letter that highlights why you might just be the person to solve their problem, if indeed they have one. Just remember that you're playing the odds here. Most of the companies you contact will not be in the market for a new CFO. But if you do happen to contact a CEO who has been contemplating a change in financial executive talent for some months, and if you have the background that will solve that firm's immediate problems and help take it to the next level, you may just be looking at your next job.

Straight Answers to Real Questions

▶ I'm a Canadian CFO Working Overseas – What Can I Earn When I Get Back Home?

Question: I'm a Canadian CPA CA working in Israel where I'm the CFO of a $200mm industrial concern with subsidiaries in Europe and Africa. I earned my CA designation with E&Y in 1998 and had six years' experience as the controller and then VP Finance of a mid-sized manufacturer before I moved overseas. I've enjoyed the eight years I've spent here but my wife and I are missing Canada (if not the winters) and want to return home. My current remuneration is a base salary (converted to CAD) of $265,000 plus a performance-based bonus that could reach 30%.

I've given myself up to a year to find a suitable position, preferably in the GTA. Some people have suggested that since I've been out of the Canadian market for so long I should consider a lesser position and a cut in pay in order to make the transition back to the Canadian market. I'd really like to move forward with my career, not backward, and earn around the same as I'm making now – is that realistic?

Answer: I don't see why not. You're a Canadian citizen with essentially the same qualifications and experience as any of your GTA-based peers in equivalent

CFO positions. In fact, I'd even make the argument that your international experience gives you a leg up on most of your peers. Most $200mm industrial companies based in the GTA will be paying their CFO something along the lines of what you're earning now, so I'd say you're right in the ballpark.

I'm guessing that the people suggesting you consider a pay cut to move back to Canada are Canadians and not Europeans or Israelis. It's an odd thing, but some people deem experience garnered outside our borders less relevant than its Canadian counterpart. Of course, you're going to have to compete on your own merits when CFO opportunities arise and the logistics of looking for a job from 9,000 km away are going to be a trial, but you should be competing on a level playing field.

4

Resumés: Stock the Shelves with the Stuff That Sells

Think about how Hollywood producers sell their movies. They take a two-hour movie and condense it down to its best two minutes. The trailer they release is intended to give the audience a good sense of what the movie's about and hopefully persuade the viewer that this is a movie that they're going to want to plunk down $15 to see. The people making the trailer know exactly who their audience is and they make sure that the bits they cram into those two minutes are going to resonate with that particular audience.

If you were a movie, what would your trailer look like? Who is your target audience and what are they going to want to see? Your resumé is your trailer and it should tell the reader a very short, coherent story of your career and be packed with highlights that are going to resonate with your particular audience.

Generally speaking, your audience is any company, large or small, that wants to hire a CFO. So the overall story you want to convey is how you progressed from being a bright young accounting professional to a full-fledged, capable, competent, inspirational financial executive. Later on in this chapter, we'll talk about specific things to include that will appeal to the biggest part of your audience, SMEs.

As you're crafting your resumé, your watchwords should be *short* and *coherent*. No one has the time to read the resumé version of *War and Peace* – keep it to two, possibly three pages. And make sure your resumé tells a logical story of progression and achievement that will make sense to the reader and keep them interested all the way through.

Don't try to cram in every little thing and don't overuse bullet points. Bullet points are useful when you're listing accomplishments, but too many bullet points make your resumé look like a grocery list. And put yourself in context – what you've done is tied in to where you did it. Tell the reader who your employers were and where you fit into the grand scheme of things. Once you've done that, you can list what you actually accomplished. For example:

Widgets International Inc. – 2005 to present

Widgets International Inc. is a TSX listed company with assets of $700 million and annual revenues of $240 million. The company has manufacturing and distribution facilities across Canada with sales offices located in France, Italy and Japan.

Vice President, Finance
Reporting to the CEO

Overseeing a staff of 30 through five managers, I am responsible for the direction and management of all corporate accounting, financial reporting, treasury, risk management and financing activities.

Selected achievements:

- Played an integral role in acquiring our biggest competitor in Western Canada, managing the valuation work, due diligence and financing activities.

- Led the completion of a preliminary offering memorandum for the company's dot.com startup business. Ultimately sold the business for a significant profit.

- Developed a monthly management reporting package using Balanced Scorecard performance management concepts providing operating executives with significantly improved management information.

As you work backward from your current employer, you should be putting in fewer details while trying not to repeat yourself. If you've already established yourself as an IT guru at ABC Company, you don't need to cover that ground again for DEF Company.

The hardest part of this exercise is unpacking 20 or 30 years of experience and achievement and deciding what goes into your resumé and what stays out. The marketing gurus in Hollywood have the same issue when they're putting together the trailer. They need to extract two minutes out of 120 and string them together in a way that will tell the story of the movie that will make their audience want to see more.

Keep in mind that a very large part of your target audience is the CEO of a small or medium-sized company and pay special attention to those skill sets or experiences that are common to the world of SMEs.

These include:

- *Working with owner-managers or entrepreneurs:* Working for a professional CEO in a well-established, large, sophisticated Canadian company is usually a very different experience than working for the person that started the business or their progeny. Owner-managers and entrepreneurs are often their own special brand of manager; it can take a lot of tact, patience and perseverance to be successful in the CFO role in one of these companies. Without making too much of a big thing out of it (after all, challenging bosses don't usually know that they're demanding), you can point out somewhere that you've had significant experience in this kind of environment and have prospered in it.

- *Information Technology (IT) experience*: In three out of five CFO searches that I undertake, information systems or, more to the point, the need for better information systems is a big factor in the search. If you have led an ERP installation or conversion and / or are very comfortable and competent in all things IT, point it out in detail and at length. Bad IT systems or an ERP implementation that has gone off the rails are major irritants to any CEO. If you can demonstrate the ability to get the company's IT matters on track, it will be of special interest to a large part of your target audience.

- *Experience working for a private equity portfolio company:* Previous experience working with a private equity firm is always a trump card when applying for a CFO position with a portfolio company. Anyone who's been the CFO of a private equity portfolio company will tell you that it's a very different experience than working for your typical owner-managers. For one thing, the private equity owners you're reporting to are as good or better with numbers as you are – they know exactly what they want out of the financials and they want it delivered accurately and on time. And since the private equity owner eventually wants to exit their investment by either going public or finding a strategic buyer, experience in quarterbacking that process makes you especially attractive to a prospective private equity employer.

- *Experience dealing with explosive growth:* When companies are experiencing explosive growth, infrastructure issues inevitably arise and are often relegated to the back burner. If these issues are left unattended, they will eventually impede the company's growth and overall success. Financial executives who have successfully dealt with these types of issues – organizational development, financing, acquisitions, controls, systems, etc. – will often find that they are real contenders for the CFO position in this kind of company.

- *Maximizing enterprise value:* Ultimately, what any owner manager wants is to maximize enterprise value. Whether they plan to stay in the business until they get carried out feet first, pass their business down to their kids or eventually sell to a strategic buyer, owner-managers want to get the most bang for their buck. If you have a proven track record of dramatically maximizing enterprise value, that should put you ahead of a lot of your competition.

Once you've written your resumé, have an impartial third party give it a read and let you know if the story you wanted to tell is coming through loud and clear.

Straight Answers to Real Questions

Linking IN

Question: I'm the CFO of a $75mm consumer products distribution company in Mississauga. I've been here eight years and, although I still enjoy my job, I feel I'm getting a bit stale and think I should start looking at the market.

My kids would tell you that I'm a classic, old-school kind of guy. I don't have a Facebook account, I've never even seen Instagram and I don't tweet (and don't know why I would ever want to). To my credit, I do have a LinkedIn account but I've barely looked at it since I set it up six or seven years ago.

Now that I'm looking for a new position, how plugged in to the whole social media thing do I need to be?

Answer: You don't need to sign up for Facebook, Twitter, Instagram or Tumblr. However, you do need to spend some time and effort on your LinkedIn profile.

If you're not on LinkedIn, you're virtually invisible to all the people that may want to contact you about a new position. And although you obviously want recruiters to see your profile, LinkedIn is also used by hiring authorities when they're deciding who they'll want to interview.

Whenever a CEO puts up a job posting for a CFO, they receive a lot of resumés. Most of those resumés will be rejected as unsuitable right away. Seven or eight resumés will be worth a hard look and the hiring authority will decide which three or four they want to interview from that group.

That CEO is likely to look you up on LinkedIn. Much of the information in your profile will be mirrored on your resume, but LinkedIn gives you an opportunity to do some self-promotion and add some pizzazz to your career summary. And don't discount the power of a good profile photograph. All other things being equal, if a hiring authority has to choose between two LinkedIn profiles where one has a photo and the other doesn't, they'll pick the person with the photo.

5

Switching Industries

One of the most frequent questions I get from financial executives looking for a new position is: Can I switch industries?

And the short answer to that question is: Yes. In fact, I would encourage financial executives to build their career in more than one industry as this will tend to increase their career options down the road.

However, there are a few factors to consider when you're contemplating a switch in industries that may impact your overall job-search strategy.

There are usually three reasons that a CFO considers changing industries. First, if they are actively on the job market, they want to increase their field of potential employers. Second, if they are gainfully and somewhat happily employed, CFOs often want to change industries simply because they've run out of technical challenges and want to re-engage in a new environment. Third, because they happen to be working in the modern-day equivalent of the buggy whip business and want to jump out of that particular industry before they get pushed.

Whatever the reason, when considering a change in industries, here are three things you should keep in mind:

1. *The economy:* Ironically, the best time to look at changing industries is when you probably aren't really motivated to make any drastic changes. A strong economy usually translates into too few good candidates for positions on offer. And within a strong economy, there are usually one or more very hot segments that are growing like a weed and crying out for qualified professionals and executives. If you suspect that you'll want or need to get out of manufacturing where you've spent the last 20 years, a booming economy is when you want to start putting feelers out.

2. *Size of company:* As discussed in Chapter 1, by the time finance and accounting professionals percolate up into VP Finance positions, they are usually working for small and medium-sized enterprises. And even though you may be in the top financial spot of an organization and a valued member of the executive team, CFOs of SMEs still need to be relatively hands-on. Aside from your financial prowess, a big part of the value-add that

you bring to the table is your knowledge of the particular company and industry you work in.

The implication of the last statement is that for the most part, SMEs tend to have a strong bias towards candidates from their own industry when recruiting a CFO. In very large organizations, it tends to be easier for top financial executives to switch industries. Typically these CFOs are more focused on strategic, organizational and finance issues than the actual nuts and bolts of the business.

That being said, there is a quirk of the SME market which proves the exception to the rule that CEOs of SMEs tend to hire from within their own industry. There's a largish subset of owner-managers that aren't all that fussed about getting operational input and just want the financial function to run smoothly with no surprises. To this segment of the market, if you've got your CPA, have been a Director of Finance or CFO before and seem like a decent person, you are a definite candidate for the position on offer, regardless of what industry you currently work in.

3. *Your ability to bring something new to the table*: Most owner-managers and CEOs of SMEs want their CFO to provide significant input into overall operations and will tend to hire someone who brings a wealth of industry experience to the table in addition to their financial expertise.

However, if you don't happen to have the

industry experience this type of CEO is looking for, you may still be a viable contender for the CFO position. Sometimes a CEO will conclude that their company could benefit from some cross-fertilization from a different industry. They know that opportunity often lies in applying old technologies to new situations or applying new technologies to old situations. If you work in an old-school industry that could teach something to a new economy company or, conversely, have knowledge of new techniques or technologies that could revitalize a mature company, you stand a pretty good chance of finding a new home (and industry) with a CEO who recognizes your unique value-add proposition.

None of the above will actually change your recruitment strategy. You should be looking at as many opportunities as present themselves, regardless of industry. However, knowing some of these factors may help you to fine-tune your approach and, at the least, help manage your expectations.

Straight Answers to Real Questions

Time Kills All Deals

Question: I've recently been interviewing with a $100mm manufacturer for a newly created Vice President, Finance position. I started the process four months ago and have had six interviews so far. I've met the CEO, his executive team, his father and brother (the company is family owned) and the firm's public accounting partner, and now they want me to meet with a firm next week to do a personality profile.

The people at this company assure me that they're very interested in me and I'm still quite interested in the position. However, this morning I got a call from a recruiter I know who wants me to meet with one of her clients tomorrow for a CFO role that sounds very intriguing. Should I hang on and see how the first position pans out or should I start to entertain other opportunities?

Answer: By all means, interview for the CFO position the recruiter called you about. Obviously, in spite of their assurances, the first firm is having some difficulty in reaching a decision. Even if you've met them six times, there's no guarantee that you're going to get the nod.

There's no downside to meeting the second firm. If the first firm you interviewed with comes through with an offer next week, you can just excuse yourself from consideration on the other CFO job. If you really like the other CFO opportunity and they come through with an offer first, all other things being equal, that's a great outcome too.

If you do decide to meet with the second firm, you should probably let them know that you're interviewing with another company. And you should definitely let the first firm know that you're considering other opportunities as well. If they're really interested in you, they'll expedite their process. If they don't hurry things along, it should tell you that maybe they're not as keen on you as you thought they were.

6

Prepping for the Interview

Taking my analogy from Chapter 4 a step further, if your resumé is the two-minute trailer of the movie that is your career, the interview is the pitch meeting. Your job is to convince the prospective employer that you're going to be an investment that's going to pay off in a big way.

So, as you prepare for an interview, start to think of yourself as a potential investment and frame your potential employer as the person making the investment – what kind of return are they going to be looking for?

This will often involve some research and deductive reasoning since most CFO job descriptions are fairly generic. These job descriptions will reference timely and accurate financial information, financial planning, budgets and forecasts, treasury operations, etc. – all of which are part and parcel of any CFO position but none of which tell you what the job is really all about.

Every CFO position is informed by the size of the company, the industry it operates in and the current SWOT situation (strengths, weaknesses, opportunities and threats). The position is also impacted by what's gone on before (does the finance group need to be re-engineered?) and the expectations of the future. There are often major IT issues that need to be addressed (in three out of five CFO searches I conduct, the lack of adequate systems are an issue). And of course, the CFO position is materially affected by the CEO's personality and the dynamic of the management team.

When I meet with a client to discuss a CFO search, this is what we talk about. Even if the client has gone through the trouble of putting together a job description, most if not all of what is listed in that document are table stakes items – they're inevitably not what the client and I end up discussing as being the drivers of success in the position.

That's the problem with boilerplate job descriptions – they don't tell the prospective candidate what's really going on with the company doing the hiring and the particular experience and skill sets required to really ace the job. And if you don't know what your potential customer (the hiring authority) is shopping for, it's very difficult to know what to pitch.

Don't assume that just because you're a seasoned CFO and your experience covers each and every bullet point in the job description that your resumé is going to wow a prospective employer. Most of the resumés that they're going to look at will touch on most if not all of the bullet points detailed in the job description. That's not actually what they're looking for. Simply put, what they're looking for is *someone who's going to solve their problem*.

So, as the prospective candidate, you've got two challenges. Challenge number one: figure out what problem(s) the prospective employer needs solved, and number two: specifically detail how you would solve the problem(s).

If you're dealing with a headhunter in looking at a specific opportunity, the first part will be easy. The headhunter should be able to give you chapter and verse on the history of the company and the specific challenges and opportunities that the company and the CFO position will be facing.

If you heard about the opportunity from a friend, you might be able to get part of the story through them, but you should also do the same kind of research you would do if you just saw the job posted on the web.

Obviously, you're going to visit the company's website and glean as much information as you can about the company's history, place in the market, management team, products, etc. Next, do a search for any press releases or announcements associated with the company or any of their top executives. You can also look up the management team on LinkedIn and see if you can pick up any additional information. Another tip is to find any industry-specific online trade magazines. These can often give you insights on what the particular issues are in that industry, companies on the move and what industry or product innovations are making the news.

While this research may not give you an exact fix on what the prospective employer may be looking for, it should give you an idea of the areas that may be of particular interest to the hiring authority. If nothing else, you'll be 90% better prepared for an interview than any of your competition.

The next step is to numerate the issues you know (or suspect) the hiring authority is particularly interested in and in detail address what you know about that issue and how you've dealt with it in the past. If you have had an in-depth briefing on the challenges facing the new CFO, you might even want to treat it as a case study and lay out how you would address those issues if you got the job.

Whatever else you learn or deduce about a position that you're going to be interviewing for, if your prospective employer is an owner-managed company, they're also going to be looking for the following traits in their next CFO:

Someone who cheerfully does what needs doing. Small company executives don't have the luxury of staffing out the many myriad problems and challenges that arise on a regular basis. CFOs may be making a presentation to their bankers one day and fixing the copier the next. In almost all small businesses, the successful CFO's philosophy will be "No job is too big, no job is too small."

Someone who parks their ego outside. Part and parcel of the "can-do" attitude is the absence of the "corner suite syndrome" some executives fall prey to. The successful CFO recognizes that everyone in the organization has an integral role to play in the company's success. They treat employees on the loading dock with the same respect as they do executives in the boardroom.

Someone who gets the big picture. In many small businesses the CFO is the right-hand person to the CEO and will be very involved in operational initiatives as well as strategic planning. Although their area of expertise may be finance, they also need to be very well versed in sales, marketing, operations and distribution.

A utility player. Small businesses often have to roll non-financial functions under the CFO. Besides overseeing the finance and accounting function, CFOs in small businesses often have responsibility for human resources, IT and general administration. And of course, any special projects that arise, such as relocating or building new facilities, will also likely fall under their purview.

Someone who'll be highly visible within the organization. Successful small business CFOs spend as little time as possible in their office. They want to get to know what's really going on in the business, so they're on the shop floor, they're getting to know the sales people and they're talking to customers and suppliers. By being highly visible and accessible, they have conversations that give them insights into the business that they wouldn't get from the financials alone.

There's an adage in sales that you should always sell benefits, not features. Features are the surface statements about your product, what it can do, its dimensions and specs, and so on. That's your resumé.

Benefits are the end result of what a product can actually accomplish for the customer. That's what this exercise is all about and what you should always be emphasizing in an interview.

Straight Answers to Real Questions

► Salary Surveys – The Real Deal or Empty Calories?

Question: I'm the Vice President, Finance for a $60mm CPG manufacturer in Vaughan. The company's been doing quite well but the owners are getting close to retirement age and are talking about looking for a strategic buyer. The new owners may want to keep me on but the odds are against it. I decided to take a look at the market. I've been here for over 10 years and, although I think I've been paid fairly, I have no idea what my real market value is.

I downloaded the most recent salary survey published by a major accounting recruitment firm and it cites the salary range for CFOs of companies with revenues of $50mm to $100mm as being between $131,750 and $177,750. How do I know where I am on that spectrum?

Answer: Unfortunately, the short answer is: You can't know. You're pinpointing a problem that is endemic to most salary surveys – the ranges they quote are too broad to be of any real use to an employer or a candidate trying to benchmark their compensation. In surveys like this, the data is usually taken from all the placements that firm made in that reporting period. The main problem with this approach is that the people being placed and the firms doing the hiring are going to cover a very wide spectrum of variables.

For instance, a manufacturing company in a mature market with no growth plans and tight margins may hire a VP Finance for a maintenance-type function at a salary of $140,000 and a 10% bonus potential. A manufacturer of a similar size just down the road that's been experiencing dramatic growth and that plans to stay on its current trajectory may pay its CFO $225,000 plus a bonus worth up to 30% of salary.

Which brings me to the other issue with salary surveys of this sort – they only reflect the salaries for the recruitment firm's recent placements. This data does not reflect the overall market. The range cited in this case suggests that $177,750 is the top end of CFO salaries for companies of this size, which is definitely not the case; the salaries are actually quite a bit higher.

The best way to get a handle on your real market value is to find someone in a similar professional situation and benchmark your employer, position and compensation against theirs. If you have pals in similar jobs, great – that's the first place you should turn. If not, consider joining a networking group for financial executives. Not only will you pick up market intelligence on compensation, you may also find the group useful in helping you find your next job.

7

Avoiding the Bad Bosses

Every now and again I'll have a finance executive ring me up and ask me to find them a new position when they've only been with their current employer for a matter of six or eight months. They're almost always well-regarded professionals who've never before precipitously jumped ship. When I ask why they want to move after such a short time, the answer is invariably the same: They were not given the full story when they joined and, in some cases, they were outright lied to during the interview process.

Of course, one could chide the finance executive for not having done enough due diligence prior to taking the job, but the real question here is why a company would fudge the truth about a position it wants to fill.

The usual reason is that the challenges associated with the position are inevitably a function of the company culture or of the hiring authority themselves. Sometimes the hiring authority intentionally glosses over problems with a position hoping against hope that the next person will be better able to cope with those particular challenges. But more commonly, the hiring authority doesn't realize that they are at the root of the problem and so the subject never actually comes up.

No two organizations are the same. Some companies have flex hours and beer bashes Friday afternoons and some companies expect their executives to put in 60-hour weeks and check in with the office when they're on vacation. Some bosses are hands-off, big-picture delegators, and some bosses are micromanagers. One is not inherently "better" than the other (Tony Hsieh of Zappos.com has a very upbeat, nurturing style; Apple's Steve Jobs was notoriously hard to work for). But hands-off, big-picture delegators know that they're hands-off, big-picture delegators. The problem is that the micromanagers often think that they're big-picture delegators too.

Everyone would be a lot better off, including and especially the hiring authority, if they hired for who they actually are, not some idealized version of who they wish they could be. A CEO who habitually puts in 60-hour weeks is never going to be happy with a Vice President, Finance who needs to be home in time for dinner with their family every night. And if a company is family owned and the entire fractious clan needs to approve any and all operational changes, then that may be a continual source of frustration for their freshly hired CFO who was given a mandate to help take the company to the next level.

CEOs can take steps to avoid this disconnect in the recruitment and hiring process. As painful as it might be, the CEO should make an honest assessment of the company's culture, the various stakeholders' needs, their own management style and the challenges associated with position. If 60-hour weeks have been the norm for the past few years, then that's part of the culture and it's not going to end anytime soon. If the company has fallen on hard times and part of the CFO's job will be to stave off anxious creditors, they should make sure prospective candidates know that up front. If the owner-manager likes to have the final say in all decisions, they should ensure that's acknowledged and factored into the recruitment and hiring process as well.

Whatever the company culture, management style or particular challenges of the position might be, companies need to recognize them up front, be prepared to articulate them openly and honestly, and factor them into the recruitment strategy.

CFOs can also take steps to avoid joining a company where they have little or no chance of success. Bad bosses and bad jobs usually radiate danger signals if you know what to look for. If anything in the interview raises red flags with you, make note and investigate further. Ask to meet with other members of the executive team. Don't just listen to the answers they give to your questions, pay special attention to how they answer. If they're guarded, uncomfortable or evasive, don't shrug it off – they're telling you something you need to pay attention to.

Do backchannel checks with people who've had dealings with the company if you can. Find previous employees on LinkedIn and send them a note asking them if they'd be willing to talk to you about their past experience.

And finally, trust your gut. If the company's been through three different CFOs in the past six years, I don't care how plausible the CEO's story is about the turnover – you're going to be on the casualty list yourself in about two years.

Straight Answers to Real Questions

Compensation Conundrum

Question: I took a pretty big drop in my base salary a few years ago in order to join a high-tech startup as its CFO. My compensation is heavily weighted towards incentives tied to company performance – base salary, plus variable pay up to 100% of salary, plus stock options.

Unfortunately, the company hasn't had the success we'd hoped for and the management team is just drawing base salaries, which in my case is $130,000. I've decided to make a move and have been looking at positions paying around $200,000 plus a bonus (which will get me back to where I should be). I'm afraid of being low-balled if and when I get to the offer stage. How do I handle the question of compensation expectations?

Answer: At your level, there shouldn't be much chance of being low-balled. Any company that tries to get away with an egregiously low offer is not a company you want to work for anyway. That being said, it's part of the negotiation process for each party to try to strike the best deal they can. Position postings usually refer to a salary range and because you're currently well below market, some prospective employers may assume that they can get by with an offer in a very low part of the range.

However, the salary range of any position is not a function of what the candidate was earning before, it's a function of how qualified they are for the job. For example, if you're moderately qualified, maybe the low end of the range is fair. If you're well qualified, you're probably in the middle to upper-middle end of the pay scale. And if you're dead-solid perfect, they could be testing the upper limits of the range.

Be frank about the circumstances leading to your current compensation and be up front about what you expect to earn with your next job. Whatever you do, don't equivocate about what you think your market value is. If you don't set an appropriate price on your services, odds are a prospective employer won't either.

8

What You Need to Know About Headhunters

The first thing you need to know about headhunters is that generally speaking, they won't be keen to meet up with you when you first reach out to them. If you've had a previous close relationship with a particular recruiter, they may be willing to have a quick meeting but, for the most part, all a headhunter wants is a copy of your resumé for their files.

Of course, once a headhunter has a position that you may be a fit for, they are going to want to meet with you. But if headhunters met with every job seeker that contacted them, they'd spend an inordinate amount of time meeting candidates that they're probably never going to place. In fact, unless for some reason your particular kind of resumé is in very high demand, the odds are against that headhunter ever phoning you at all.

The second thing you need to know about headhunters is that they come in two very distinct flavours – placement agencies and executive search firms. I realize that this distinction is often lost on the general market because just about every placement agency that works on mid- to senior-level positions markets itself as an executive recruiter. The key distinction is that placement agencies work on a contingency-fee basis and executive recruiters work on a retained basis.

If you're going to talk to some recruiters, you should know how these recruitment firms work and manage your expectations accordingly.

Placement Agencies

The value proposition of placement agencies is that they have qualified applicants that are immediately available for interviewing. They make extensive use of job postings and networking sites to acquire their stock and are constantly triaging and assessing applicants to ensure that they have an adequate supply of ready product. The applicants they represent are usually very active in the market, so agencies need to aggressively market their services to ensure that they have a constant stream of orders to match to their applicants. Since placement agencies work on a contingency-fee basis (usually non-exclusive), they can't afford to spend too much time or effort on any one assignment.

In the placement industry model, the odds of being paid decrease as a function of time. A placement agency is incented to try to fill a job order quickly and then move on. It doesn't make economic sense for an agency to invest a lot of time and effort into any one search as the client is just as likely to hire from a competing agency. If a placement agency is given an exclusive assignment, it will make the extra effort to tap into its database and do research on sites like LinkedIn in order to do some actual headhunting on the client's behalf. But since there's still no guarantee of payment, there are limits to how long and how hard an agency will be willing to work on a contingency assignment.

You should also be aware that the sweet spot for practically every placement agency is the junior to middle part of the market (which includes controllers). So if you responded to a placement agency's job board posting for a CFO, that posting may be the only CFO job that placement agency works on that year. That being said, since that placement agency doesn't do much work in the CFO space, it probably doesn't have a large stock of good CFO resumés. If the agency lands another CFO position to work on, all other things being equal, the odds are fairly good that you'll get a call.

Executive Search Firms

The value proposition of executive search firms is that they have sophisticated research and recruitment capabilities that allow them to conduct searches across the country or around the world. High-end executive search is a high-cost / high-service / low-volume business. Their fees are based on 30%–35% of total remuneration with add-ons and chargebacks that can take the overall fee to over 40%. Search firms spend considerable time and effort to acquire their clients, and they work very hard to keep these clients happy. Executive recruiters are usually very experienced professionals and the focus of their efforts lies in making sure that their research and recruiting result in the best executive and cultural fit for their client. Since search firms are always paid (and paid very well), they focus on quality of results, not volume of work.

These firms typically have internal specialists in specific industry verticals, not functional verticals. They may have partners who specialize in retail, transportation and consumer packaged goods, but they probably won't have someone who specializes in financial executives. That being said, if any of their retail, transportation or CPG clients are looking for a CFO, they will get the search.

If an executive search firm is conducting a search for a CFO and you happen to be in its database or see the job posted on LinkedIn, there are still a number of barriers to overcome before you get a shot at the job. Your profile will be one of a 100 to 150 other profiles that the headhunter is considering.

And even if you make the cut at this stage and get invited in for an interview with the recruiter, it doesn't mean that you'll be presented to the client. After all, a headhunter's job is to present the best possible person for the position and that entails triaging all available candidates to a short list that best meets the client's criteria. Even if you get all the way to the final short list, if the recruiter is any good, they will ensure that their client is looking at least three or four other candidates who are just as qualified.

The final thing you need to know about head-hunters is that you probably won't get your next job through one. If and when a headhunter approaches you on a position, put your best foot forward but, in the initial stages of your job search, just reach out to the headhunters you think may be in a position to help you and don't overinvest in this part of your job-hunting strategy.

As I've discussed earlier in this book, the main reason you won't find your next job through a recruiter is that only a small fraction of the available Director of Finance or CFO jobs in small and mid-sized companies are listed with recruitment firms.

The majority of SMEs that are recruiting for their top financial position rely on networking and word of mouth to source their candidates. Whether or not this is the way to go is a matter of some debate, but the fact remains that this is how most of the smaller companies conduct their recruiting.

Don't assume that just because the headhunter community knows that you're looking for a new job that this will be your main source of new opportunities. The reality is that calls from headhunters will range from few and far between to nil and you should be proactive in finding your next opportunity through your own efforts.

Straight Answers to Real Questions

▶ Should I Take a Contract?

Question: I've been unemployed for almost four months and, although I've had a couple of interviews, there's no reason to believe that I'll be gainfully employed again anytime soon. I'm thinking about hiring myself out on contract, if for no other reason than to get out of the house. I've been told that having contract positions on my resumé will be a turnoff for potential full-time employers – is this true?

Answer: I actually think that if you've been on the street for an extended length of time and you *don't* have any contract work on your resumé, it's a potential turnoff for prospective employers. Just because you've taken on a couple of contracts, it doesn't mean that you're now a contractor. It just means that you've been keeping busy, staying productive and, more to the point, keeping your cash flow flowing.

The only thing to keep in mind is that you structure each long-term contract so that you can extricate yourself in a reasonable time frame with notice. Ideally your exit time frame will be one month because any company that hires you as their full-time CFO will expect that the successful candidate will give their current employer one month's notice. A two-month notice period is stretching it but is often acceptable to prospective employers. Anything more than two months becomes problematic. Of course, your other option is to focus on short-term contracts so the notice issue doesn't come into play.

Depending on market conditions, it's entirely possible that you may be a year or more between full-time jobs. Twelve months is a long time to go without a pay cheque and a gap that long doesn't look good on your resumé.

9

Putting It All Together

Your level of commitment to the job-hunting process will be a function of your current circumstance. Someone who's been on the street for a few months will have a whole different approach than someone who'd like to make a change in the next two years or so.

For most CFOs, especially CFOs who have some urgency around finding a new position, job hunting is more than a bit of a grind. In terms of underlying principles and mechanics, job hunting is essentially an exercise in selling, something most CFOs have no experience with.

What most people don't know about selling (including most sales people) is that the key to success in sales isn't how compelling you are in the meeting. The key to success in selling lies in the preparation that leads to the meetings.

Sales is a numbers game. And in almost any field of sales, the numbers that lead to success are actually quite large. Some sales people will typically make 50 or more cold calls a day. They cheerfully make those calls knowing that by the end of the week the 250 calls they made will result in 25 actual introductory conversations. Those 25 conversations would, in turn, translate into five meetings. And they know that if they make five presentations, at least one of them will turn into a sale.

These sales people aren't guessing and they're not wishing. Companies keep stats on these ratios and all have their variation of the formula: x cold calls = y conversations = z presentations = # sales.

The hardest part of the process isn't making the calls (although that is pretty hard to novice sales people). The hardest part is putting together a big enough list of quality prospects to call.

Just like sales people, you need to work the numbers. Start by putting together a list of everyone and anyone who's in a position to hear about opportunities and refer your name. Send them a note, call them up and, if at all possible, try to get in front of them. Just be aware that public accounting partners, bankers and lawyers get approached all the time by people trying to access their particular markets and don't be offended if they're reluctant to agree to a meeting.

Next, really take some time to do the research we talked about in Chapter 3. Try to come up with as large a list as you possibly can. The more companies you approach, the better your chances of success. Some of the prospect companies on your list are going to be there for obvious reasons and some are going to be a bit more of a stretch. But you'll need a list of 50 to 100 prospects if you want to give yourself a decent chance of winning in this particular numbers game. If you had to manually type each and every one of the cover letters and resumés on an old IBM Selectric, you'd probably be reluctant to go through the effort for the more doubtful prospects. But in the world we live in today, the incremental effort to send out 50 resumés versus 20 resumés isn't really a factor.

You may have just blanched when you read 50 prospects in the paragraph above. But that's the kind of numbers we're talking here if you're really motivated and want to make headway in your job search. If you're research actually turns up 100 prospective companies where you should send your resumé, all the better. In the world of job hunting, less isn't more – more is more.

Just like successful sales people, it pays to have an action plan and set yourself quotas. It's entirely reasonable to expect that in the first month or two of your search you should be able to generate a list of 10 people in a position to refer you to opportunities.

You should also be able to put together a list of at least 50 companies where you can send your resumé. Try to get one meeting with one referral source a week and send out at least 10 resumés with cover letters a week.

There are literally thousands of SMEs in the GTA and thousands more across Canada, and the majority of them have the CFO position on their organizational chart. If you've got the time (and the perseverance), you'll never run out of companies where you can market yourself.

Straight Answers to Real Questions

▶ Bridesmaid's Blues

Question: Two weeks ago, I had the final of four interviews for a VP Finance role at a mid-sized public company. A few days later, the recruiter I was working with told me the company had gone with another candidate who was a "better fit." Yesterday, the recruiter called again saying that the job was still available, the company was still very interested in me and would like to meet me one more time. Frankly, I'm of two minds about this. I really like the company and the challenge of the position, but I don't like the idea of being someone's second choice. If I wasn't the best fit the first time around, what does that say about my prospects with this company if they decide to offer me the job?

Answer: Trivia question: What do Sean Connery, Judy Garland and Humphrey Bogart have in common?

They were all second choices for the roles that made them famous (James Bond, Dorothy in *The Wizard of Oz*, Rick in *Casablanca*).

In a good short list, the hiring authority likes all of the candidates and likes one enough to invite them back for second and third interviews. In a great short list, the hiring authority likes all of the candidates and likes two of them enough to invite them both back for more interviews. Those two candidates may go through three or four interviews before the company eventually makes their decision. I've been privy to the decision-making process on finalist candidates many times and I can tell you that the process can be torturous. The hardest decisions are when the company has to decide between two great candidates that are so close in terms of professional qualifications and cultural fit that the hiring authority might as well toss a coin.

If you made it to the fourth round of interviews, it tells me that you were part of a great short list (kudos to your recruiter), and that if the other candidate was the better fit, it was only by the smallest margin. So, if I were you, I wouldn't be concerned that I wasn't picked first time out; I'd be grateful the other candidate backed out and that I was being asked back to the dance.

Afterword

Everyone's probably heard the old saying that looking for a job is a full-time job. It's not. A full-time job is a full-time job. Looking for a job may seem to be full time at first, but sooner or later, full days of job hunting become half days of job hunting and then eventually a couple of mornings of job-hunting activity a week.

When it comes to job hunting, I prefer this Wayne Gretzky quote: "You miss one hundred percent of the shots you don't take."

Effective job hunting is all about making opportunities to tell your story as often as you can.

Don't be discouraged if all your activity isn't turning into interviews right away. Job hunting is largely about being in the right place at the right time. And the more resumés you send out, the better the chances of your resumé landing on the desk of someone who happens to be in the market for a CFO.

You may not get any interviews in the first three months and then have five interviews in month four.

There's no way of predicting how your job-search campaign is going to play out. Just keep at it and have faith that your efforts are going to result in the CFO position you've been looking for.

One last word of advice – as soon as you start getting the sense that you'll need to make a move in the distant future, you may want to start actively looking at the market. It may happen that the right position crops up a bit before you're really ready to move, in which case you'll have a difficult decision to make. But it's always better to be in a position of dealing with untimely options than having no options at all when you really need one.

Appendix A

More Straight Answers to Real Questions

▶ *Time Is(n't) On My Side*

Question: I was having lunch with a couple of pals, both of whom are on the market for a new position, and the subject of position tenure came up. One of my friends, Andrew, is the CFO of an industrial parts distribution company that's just been acquired by an American private equity firm. He joined the firm right out of public accounting and he's been there for about 20 years.

My other friend, Grace, is VP Finance of a civil engineering firm. In the course of her 25-year career, she's worked for six different companies in three different industries, and her average tenure is about four years. All other things being equal, how does the market regard someone who's been at the same place for 20-plus years versus someone who's moved around quite a bit?

Answer: There's no one correct answer to your friends' question. On one hand, if Andrew has been at the same company in the same industry for 20-odd years, I'm sure he knows that particular business and industry inside out. And of course, he's demonstrated that he's a very loyal, stable employee. So if a prospective employer is in that same industry, especially if that company is a direct competitor of Andrew's current employer, Andrew should have the inside track on that CFO position.

But if a prospective employer is in a different industry, someone with Grace's resumé may be perceived to be the better candidate. Since Grace has worked for six companies in three different industries, she will probably have seen a much greater variety of issues over the course of her career. Andrew's knowledge may be much deeper, but Grace will probably have a greater breadth of knowledge. So if Andrew and Grace are competing for the same job with a company in a different industry than Andrew's current employer, all other things being equal, Grace will probably get the nod.

Sometimes You're Hot, Sometimes You're Not

Question: I'm the VP Finance of a $25mm printing and digital media company. I've been with this company for just over six years and, some time ago, I decided it was time to start to look at the market. When I made the decision to make a move I reached out to all the headhunters I've dealt with over the years and sent them my resumé. I'm a CPA, CA and I like to think that I've got a pretty marketable resumé, but it's been over six months and none of the recruiters I contacted have called me with a position. For that matter, none of them wanted to interview me when I reached out to them.

Twenty years ago when I registered with recruiters, they all wanted to meet with me and I got my first three jobs through them. If I was such a hot commodity before, what's going on now?

Answer: There are actually a few things going on here, none of which are necessarily a function of you (I'll have to take your word that you're as marketable as you say you are), but are rather a function of the place in the market you currently occupy.

First of all, there's always a market for recently designated CPAs. In fact, for many placement agencies in the finance and accounting market, this is where they really live. When you were a fresh-faced young CA, any and all of the recruiters you reached out to would have multiple jobs on the books calling for people like you. So naturally, they all wanted to interview you and it's no surprise that you ended up getting placed a few times this way.

Fast forward to now, the market is materially different for you. At your level, your shelf life as a job seeker isn't a month or two. Unless you luck out, it's at least six months and more probably, eight months to a year.

As I've referenced in previous blogs, headhunters don't see most of the VP Finance and CFO jobs in the small and medium-sized enterprise market that may be out there. The go-to recruitment tool for SMEs is word of mouth. And if networking doesn't work, they'll take a chance with posting their CFO position on a job board. I'd guestimate that less than 15% of the CFO positions available at any time are in the hands of recruiters, so it's not actually that surprising that you're not hearing from the head-hunters you're registered with.

And finally, the reason none of the headhunters wanted to meet with you this time around is that they know that the odds of them seeing a job for you in the next six months are exceedingly low. No doubt all of the recruiters have entered you in their data-base and will certainly interview you if they actually have a job for you, but there isn't really a compelling reason to meet with you at this stage of the game.

► Should I Stay or Should I Go?

Question: I'm the CFO of an owner-managed cosmetics manufacturer here in Mississauga. I've been here for over nine years and I'm wondering if I should start looking at the market. It's not that I'm unhappy; I like my boss, the work's interesting and everything's humming along pretty smoothly.

My concern is that if I stay too much longer that it may be difficult to find another job if and when I need to make a move (I've heard that if you stay too long in one place that you're less marketable). I don't have any reason to think that I'll need to look at the market anytime soon, but my boss will be 60 next year and I wouldn't be shocked if he decided to sell out and move south in the next five or 10 years.

Do you think putting myself on the market is a good move or do you think I should I stay where I am?

Answer: I would say that the answer to your question is: Both. Put yourself on the market but stay where you are. First of all, if you decide that you're officially in play as of today, it's not like the phone's going to start ringing off the hook. Someone at your level can reasonably expect that it takes eight months to a year to find a new position (in some cases, people find that it can take up to two years). And that's someone who's really motivated to make a move, which you're not. Positions that you're going to be a good fit for and, more importantly, interested in, will be few and far between.

Since you're in a comfortable position right now, you're not going to move for just any position. In fact, you're only going to move for a position that is materially better than what you've got now. For you, whether or not you make a move will be self-selecting. If you don't see anything really good, stay where you are but keep your eyes open. You won't move for something that's only somewhat better than your current situation. You'll only move if you see something that's just so good that you just have to take it. So you really have nothing to lose and quite a bit to gain by putting yourself on the market.

Job Market to CFO: "It's Not You, It's Me."

Question: I've been actively on the market now for a little over six months and I'm starting to get a bit discouraged. It's not like I haven't had any action, I've actually been on five interviews through headhunters over the past few months and I've come in second each time. I think I've got a solid resumé – I've done stints as a CFO in three different entrepreneurial companies in high-tech manufacturing and software engineering and have a proven track record of driving results. Does the fact that I've been the bridesmaid five times instead of the bride mean that I may not be as hot a commodity as I assumed I was?

Answer: Without having met you or knowing anything more than what you just told me, I can tell you that you're a pretty hot commodity – probably just as good as you think you are. How do I know that? You've been out on five interviews through headhunters in the past few months. In order to get to the interview stage through a headhunter, whose job it is to scope out the market and come up with the best possible candidates, you had to beat out possibly hundreds of other potential candidates.

That's the good news. The bad news is that you wouldn't be the only strong candidate the headhunter sent out. If they were doing their job properly, they would have had their clients interview at least four other candidates, and each of the other candidates would have been just as qualified as you.

When a company interviews five good candidates, who they end up hiring isn't usually a matter of who's got the best resumé. It's a combination of any number of factors, tangible and intangible, that lead a company to pick one candidate over all the others. So the fact that you're coming in second isn't a function of you, it's just a function of luck.

By the way, five tends to be a magic number in recruiting. Companies usually need to see five candidates before they're comfortable in making a decision and candidates usually need to go on five interviews before they land a job. So it just could be that the next company you interview with ends up being your next employer.

Covering Cover Letters

Question: I'm a CFO in the food service business and I've just started to look around for a new position. I haven't looked for a new job in quite a few years and I've been asking my pals for input on the best way to present myself to prospective employers.

Some of my friends have advised me to draft a new cover letter with every resumé I send out, specifically detailing why I'm a good fit for the position I'm applying to. It seems like a lot of work – what do you think?

Answer: It actually depends on the circumstance in which you're sending out your resumé. Are you applying to an ad or online posting? Or are you sending your resumé to someone on spec? Or do you have the inside track on a CFO opening?

If you're applying to an ad or online posting, it's just good manners to include a cover letter. Personally, I tend to gloss over cover letters and go straight into the resumé. If it isn't obvious from the resumé why someone is a fit for the particular position they're applying to, anything the candidate may have included in their cover letter probably isn't going to change my mind. That being said, being a headhunter, I'm in the business of parsing resumés; someone with less experience in reading resumés may find the additional information in a cover letter useful when deciding who to interview. So if you're sending your resumé to a headhunter, you can get away with a boilerplate cover letter. If you're sending your resumé directly to the hiring authority, you may want to highlight the skill sets and experience that you think are relevant to the position you're applying for.

If you're sending your resumé to someone on spec or if you have the inside track on a CFO position, it's definitely worthwhile to include a position-specific cover letter with your resumé. When crafting the cover letter, don't just reiterate what's already in your resumé. Do some research on the company you're applying to and specifically address the challenges and opportunities that you think will resonate the most with that audience.

Why I Don't Like Functional Resumés

Question: I'm currently the VP Finance of a mid-sized auto parts manufacturer with over 25 years' experience behind me. I haven't really been on the job market but I was recently approached by a head-hunter about a really interesting CFO position with a PE-owned company in the auto parts industry with some real upside potential.

I haven't had to write a resumé in a lot of years and am of two minds on which resumé format to go for. In the past I had a traditional resumé with a chronological listing of all my employers along with related accomplishments. This time out, I'm thinking of going with a functional resumé where I list my skill sets and accomplishments up front and then summarize my work history at the bottom of my resumé. Do you have any preferences in resumé formats?

Answer: I understand the appeal of the functional resumé. In this format, you can parse your many and varied different skill sets and accomplishments in one fell swoop and avoid having to repeat yourself on your duties in each different position.

That being said, I don't like functional resumés for a number of reasons. First and foremost is that functional resumés don't accomplish the first objective of any resumé, which is to tell a story. Your list of skill sets and accomplishments don't really have much meaning if they're not in context of the company and position in which you developed these skills. In the functional format, the reader has a very hard time getting a clear picture of how your career has developed.

A well-written, chronological resumé tells a story. The reader gets a good sense of who the candidate is today and, just as importantly, the reader also knows how they got there. With a chronological resumé, the reader doesn't have to work too hard to get a good picture of what the candidate is all about. Just keep in mind that if the hiring authority (or head-hunter) is reading your resumé, they're reading a bunch of other resumés as well. If the other person's resumé is easier to understand or puts their relevant accomplishments in a better context, everything else being equal, that person gets the interview and your functional resumé goes back into the pile.

I'll Take Door Number Three

Question: I'm the Director of Finance of a specialty foods distributor in Mississauga and I've recently concluded that I need to get my resumé together and start putting some feelers out on the market. It's not urgent, but I'm getting the sense that my company's owners are starting to think about finding a strategic buyer, and I don't want to take a chance of being a casualty of any future transition.

I've been advised that since I'm going to be on the job market that I need to update my LinkedIn profile. I've been working on my profile, filling in the blanks and beefing up my current and previous positions and, according to LinkedIn, my profile strength is now "Expert" – up from "Beginner" when I started this exercise.

If I want to get to "All-Star" status, I need to add a profile picture. Which raises two questions. Do I really need a profile picture and, if so, do you have any tips for me?

Answer: The short answer to your first question is: Absolutely, positively, yes! The majority of prospective employers (and 100% of headhunters) are going to check you out on LinkedIn even if they already have your resumé. And if you have a good profile picture, it increases your chances of an interview, especially if the hiring authority has to pick between you and someone with a similar background who doesn't have a profile picture.

As to tips on profile pictures, your goal is to appear trustworthy, competent and likeable. Needless to say, you probably don't want a smart phone pic – get it done by a professional or someone who has a real camera and knows how to use it.

For the actual photo, experts recommend that you smile with your teeth (close mouthed smiles make you half as likeable apparently), dress for success (suits raise perceived competence and influence), make eye contact with the camera and stick with a head and shoulders or head to waist shot.

Your profile picture matters. Studies show that it only takes one-tenth of a second for someone to draw conclusions about you based on your photo – make sure that they draw the right conclusions.

Hobson's Choice

Question: I'm an experienced financial executive, with over 20 years of industry experience since getting my CA designation. My last position was CFO of a $100mm logistics company, which was sold a year ago to a strategic buyer in the U.S. I stayed on for a while to help with the transition but my position was eliminated and I've been on the job market for the past six months.

I recently interviewed for a position as VP Finance of a logistics / transportation firm and I think I've got a pretty good shot at this one. My issue is with the scope of the position. The firm has revenues of about $20mm and seems to be pretty happy with their market position. The company has no real plans to grow and the position on offer seems kind of routine – not nearly as challenging as the position I most recently held.

The remuneration of the position is somewhat less than what I was making before but that doesn't really concern me that much. My question is: Should I opt for the somewhat boring bird in the hand or hold out for the more interesting and remunerative bird that's still in the bush?

Answer: You pose a very tough and very common question – one that CFOs who've been on the market any length of time wrestle with all the time. And I'm not in a position to offer you a definitive answer. I can, however, point to some of the factors you should consider as you work your way through the decision-making process.

1. *Stage of career:* If you were in the final stage of your career (which I suspect you're not), taking a less challenging position is not necessarily a bad thing. You may not be using all of your bandwidth at work but that also means that you can probably clear your desk by 5:00pm every night and even play hooky on occasion to work on your golf game.

   However, if you're mid-career with lots of miles still on the tires, you're probably going to be bored within nine months and really bored within two years. This will probably put you in the market again sooner than you'd like. And by virtue of the fact that you'd be in a lesser position at lesser pay, you'll be fortunate if your next job after this is as challenging and as well paid as the position you held with your $100mm logistics employer.

2. *Financial situation:* If you're in your 40s, you've probably got significant financial obligations that you readily serviced when you were a fully employed CFO. It's common for CFOs to be on the market for 12 months or more, so you could very conceivably still be unemployed five months (or more) from now. Most CFOs in your position have a decent severance package and can ride out a year of being on the market. Others are not so lucky and the lack of cash flow does eventually come into play.

3. *Market conditions:* You don't mention what part of the country you hail from but I'm going to assume that you're somewhere in the GTA. This is good thing if you're looking for a job. The GTA (and Golden Horseshoe Region) is a very large, diversified market. Even if the general economy is slow, there are always economic hot spots in the GTA and CFO jobs to be found. If, however, you're in a smaller or less heterogeneous market and if times happen to be tough where you are, CFO jobs will be very hard to find.

4. *Contract prospects:* You may want to consider the contract market as a placeholder until you find the job you really want. Being on contract pays the bills

and gives you the time to continue your job-hunting efforts without compromising yourself. In terms of prospective employers, having a contract gig on your resumé is a better option than a full-time job that makes it look like you're going backward in your career.

As I said, this is a tough and very personal decision – there's definitely no one correct answer. If you are in your late 50s with five kids in university and out of work in Calgary when the price of a barrel of crude is hovering around $30, taking the lesser job is probably the right call. If, however, you're in your 40s, in good financial shape and live in the GTA, the better bet may be to try to get some contract work and hold out for the job you really want.

Appendix B
About Osborne Financial Search

Online recruitment tools like LinkedIn have dramatically decreased the cost and increased the speed of candidate research and recruitment for anyone who cares to use them. And with the current extent of connectivity (do you know anyone who isn't on LinkedIn?) and freely available information on the web, in theory, anyone who looks hard enough should be able to identify any potential candidate they want.

Because people are the product, a certain degree of variability will always be part of the recruitment process. However, there's no reason why the recruitment of finance and accounting professionals shouldn't be placed on the same footing as any other professional practice.

When someone works with any other professional services firm, the service that firm performs will be predictable in terms of professional standards, project timelines and costs. Anyone involved in talent acquisition should be able to avail themselves of the same standard of predictability of professionalism, timelines and costs from the recruitment firm they decide to work with.

A New Model for Recruiting Financial Executives

We've developed a value-for–money-based recruitment strategy for financial executives that takes the guesswork out of the hiring process. Our clients know at the beginning of each search what the engagement is going to cost, how long it's going to take and what the expected outcomes will be.

Our strategy takes advantage of the cost effectiveness of online recruitment tools and couples it with our extensive market knowledge of the finance and accounting market. We charge on an hourly rate basis and the end fee is a function of how much time and effort we need to invest in the project, not the remuneration of the candidate hired. In every case, the client receives the short list they asked for and the fee charged will be significantly less than what they would pay a traditional recruitment firm.

Like any other professional services firm, the work we perform is completely documented, transparent and accountable to our clients. We want our clients to hire the right candidate, and we want them to have the assurance that they've hired the best candidate possible.

If you would like more information on our firm, email me at lance@osbornefinancialsearch.com or call me at 416 567-7782.